# Contents

# Foreword

'If you're going on an assertiveness course,' a headmaster once said to a strong willed young teacher, 'then I'm going to self-defence!'

Some people have the good fortune to be born with all the confidence in the world, but many of us either transparently lack confidence or just about manage to put up a thin veneer. Even boundless confidence can sometimes be misplaced.

How much more comfortable we are when we can muster the right degree of confidence in any situation – neither relegating ourself to being a door-mat nor stooping to rudeness and unwarranted aggression. Most important, thoroughly assured people have the edge on the rest of us in their ability to give their best at work, or amongst family and friends, and in the community. They work wonders in making others feel more confident and capable, an essential part of the job for any of us who are responsible for maximising other people's performance.

The Industrial Society's very practical book will help to remove a very real barrier for many people in releasing their full potential – to the advantage of themselves and others.

Yvonne Bennion
Division Director

# Section One

# The Approach

Assertiveness is about:

- taking responsibility for yourself and being in control of yourself
- deciding what you want out of any given situation
- listening to others and understanding their feelings, wants and positions
- finding mutually acceptable solutions.

It is founded on the principle that you can learn a set of skills and techniques that help you to act over feelings so that you express your point effectively without being overcome by your emotions. Whenever you feel anxious, or out of control of a situation, by practising these skills you can stay in charge of yourself and retain your self-esteem.

Assertiveness is about identifying goals, expressing wants and feelings while respecting the feelings and wants of others. Being in charge and dealing with feelings of anxiety, and as a result building your confidence, is a primary part of assertiveness. Another essential element of the behaviour is open, honest and direct communication.

Assertiveness is useful in the following situations:

- dealing with conflict
- negotiation
- leadership and motivation
- giving and receiving feedback
- co-operative working
- being heard in meetings.

*"The right to choose* not *to assert yourself."*

The aim is to establish and protect your self-esteem, so that you can communicate clearly with colleagues, undertake fair and successful negotiation, and stay in control during situations of conflict. It is a method which can make you more effective in your working life, so that you need not resort to aggression, sarcasm, or deviousness, all of which can disrupt good working relationships and waste a lot of energy. Use of assertiveness methods for even some proportion of the time is economic of energy, burning up less in anger, frustration, and anxiety and leaving more available for positive purposes.

Using assertiveness enables you to develop confidence which will enhance your ability to progress in your career. Successful progression often rests on recognising your own ability to do an effective job and on appreciating the skills of colleagues.

As a result of being clear about your wants and abilities, you become more clear about what your scope really could be. With your increased self-esteem you do not miss opportunities through undervaluing your own skills and experience, nor do you feel threatened by other people's achievements. In addition, it can 'un-stick' working relationships that have become 'fixed' in an unsatisfactory pattern.

Delegates who have attended assertiveness courses have made comments like these:

*'I have developed an ability to set limits on how much work I take on. I seem to have found the right way now to say "no" to my boss in a way that regulates my workload to an achievable amount without her interpreting it as me being unco-operative.'*

*'I have had a very difficult relationship with a colleague, and at times I have felt really distressed by it. By going on an assertiveness course, I found a different way of dealing with her which got me out of my alternating defensive/aggressive reactions. Things have changed for the better, although I know we'll never be great friends.'*

*'I have found it easier to deal with the continual undercurrent of sexual innuendo in the office.'*

*'I am very pleased with how I coped with an angry and abusive client the other day. I managed both to stop him using foul language and to work out a compromise solution with him.'*

When the Pepperell Unit began running assertiveness courses the majority of delegates applying were women – since being listened to, increasing confidence and a sense of self-worth, and taking more positions of managerial power, are clearly-perceived needs and aims for many working women. However, in recent months the balance has shifted to 50:50 male:female applicants as more men recognise that an effective personal style without bluster, sexism or a patronising manner will be essential for their success in the 1990s.

The core of the technique consists of:

- clear formulation of your aims and objectives
- honest and direct speaking
- showing you understand the other person's point of view
- feeling able to stand your ground when that is essential to you, and being flexible when that is appropriate.

What you gain is:

- a sense of perspective
- an increase in self-knowledge
- a decrease in insecurity
- a clearer self-image.

# Section Two

# Preparing the Ground

## Starting from a strong place

In many schools, families and corporate cultures we are not encouraged to evaluate ourselves. It may feel dangerous at first to assess yourself and your skills, but this is the first step in developing a fundamental self-esteem. It may feel arrogant or bigheaded to notice that you are good at something, and you may feel you have to pretend that any ability you have is just 'lucky' or 'accidental'. Acknowledging your skills in any other way may be considered in extremely poor taste. We rely on parents, teachers, partners, and superiors at work for judgement of our efforts and suffer depression when criticised, and an unrealistic 'high' when praised.

While of course there may be technical, organisational and personal elements of your work on which you need feedback you also need to develop an ability to have a clear idea of what your *own* opinion of your work/yourself is.

It is important to keep other people's view of you in

perspective, however influential they are. Your own assessment must ultimately be your most reliable gauge of performance and progress. For example, if a superior criticises a piece of work which you believe *was* competent, although you may have to undertake changes in the work you do not have to agree with the evaluation or allow it to undermine you.

Here are some simple exercises to re-form your ability to assess yourself. They may feel artificial at first, but bear in mind that you are using them to find new ways of thinking. For some exercises you will need a partner. Choose someone who appreciates your desire to become more effective and confident, and supports you. (Not everybody has an interest in you changing and developing either in your career or as a person; make sure you choose someone who does.)

Active listening is the key to these exercises. When you are in the listening role, maintain eye contact and give support but do not introduce your own ideas and opinions. Your rôle is to help the speaker to work out what she thinks and wants, not to discuss your views.

## Exercise 1

With your partner, talk about yourself for a (timed) period of four minutes. Say only positive things about yourself. Do not worry if you need to leave pauses between sentences. Notice what is happening in your muscles and to your breathing. After the allotted time, change rôles and repeat. After your partner has spoken positively about her/himself share with each other how it felt to do this exercise. Notice whether it would have been easier or more difficult to hold forth about your weaknesses for four minutes! Notice whether you felt an urge to undercut your positive statements:

*'I'm very good at organising conferences – but then I've been doing that sort of stuff for years and years so I should be, shouldn't I?'*

*'I'm good at motivating my staff, but it just sort of comes naturally to me'.*

*'I'm good at learning new skills, but then I'm rotten at passing them on to other people'.*

Comment on whether you held your breath or clenched your hands or toes. Mention anything else you noticed.


## Exercise 2

With a partner, take it in turns for five minutes to say sentences beginning *'I'm very good at ...'.* Consciously make eye contact with your partner while you say your sentence, keep your words slow and your breath steady. Do not worry if there are pauses. Afterwards, share how it felt to say out loud what your strengths and skills are.


## Exercise 3

If you are entering a challenging situation like a job interview, a difficult meeting with a client, or a meeting with colleagues which you suspect will be acrimonious, it can be useful to remind yourself of your strengths.

If you have done Exercises 1 and 2 you will have begun to acknowledge the skills and strengths you already have. Is there a quality or an achievement of which you feel particularly proud? It may or may not have arisen in the working sphere; it may be an act of personal endurance or courage just as easily as a professional qualification or an exciting project you took to a successful conclusion. Choose whatever feels most important to you at the moment. Keep it, as it were, in your pocket, and if you begin to feel inadequate because of what is happening in your meeting or interview, remind yourself of that sense of achievement and notice that it makes you feel more in control.

*"… it can be useful to remind yourself of your strengths."*

'Whenever someone's having a go at me here I remind myself of the complicated link-up job I did with America earlier this year – it worked out well because of the effort I put in. It is clear to me that I am not a fool.'

'I was dealing with a man who was both very clever and extremely forceful. I was beginning to feel insubstantial and silly, but it suddenly came into my mind how extremely brave I had been in childbirth. I felt I had both feet on the ground again. I looked him squarely in the eyes and carried on.'

*'I remind myself that I got through my engineering training and my first two years as a civil engineer in a predominantly male environment, and am making as good progress as any of my peers.'*

Developing the habit of noticing your achievements, whether small or large, will make it easier for you to believe in yourself as an effective person.

# Starting from a fair place

### Exercise 4

In discussion with a partner or a group, or working on your own, see if you can evolve a 'bill of rights' – specifications of what you feel the rights of both parties in any situation are. When you have done so, look at the one below and consider where you agree or disagree with it. Remember that the 'bill of rights' reflects the responsibilities you owe to others and also the behaviour you believe is owed to you.

### Bill of Rights

Everyone has:

- the right to be treated with respect
- the right to have and express her/his own opinions and feelings
- the right to be listened to and taken seriously
- the right to set her/his own priorities
- the right to say "no" without feeling guilty
- the right to ask for what she/he wants
- the right to ask for information from professionals
- the right to make mistakes
- the right to choose *not* to assert oneself.

Discuss, or if working alone take some time to reflect on, any items that seem particularly surprising or important to you. Think yourself into both the rôle of *receiver* and of *giver* of the 'rights'. Notice the last item – 'the right to choose *not* to assert oneself' – assertiveness is not some kind of behavioural keep-fit that you are supposed to do all the time, it is intended to make life less and not more stressful. There are times when you may not want to expend the energy, take risks or spend time being assertive. That is perfectly all right.

# Section Three

# The Basic Stances

There are four basic 'types' of behaviour, including the assertive mode: different sorts of language and behaviour are characteristic of each.

*Aggressive* behaviour is:

- frightening, threatening, loud
- willing to achieve goals at the expense of others
- out to 'win'
- defensive, belligerent
- explosive, unpredictable.

People on the receiving end of aggressive behaviour feel:

- defensive, aggressive
- hurt
- resentful
- afraid.

Mistakes and problems do not get reported to an aggressive

person in case they 'blow up'. Colleagues are afraid of being railroaded, exploited or humiliated.

*Non-assertive or passive* behaviour is:

- opting out
- avoiding confrontation
- finding difficulty in taking responsibility or decisions
- feeling like a 'victim'
- blaming others for events
- being apologetic and refusing compliments.

People working with someone being non-assertive or passive feel:

- exasperated
- guilty
- resentful
- frustrated.

'Passive' behaviour is marked by a martyr-like attitude and a refusal to try out initiatives which might improve things. Colleagues resent the aura of low energy surrounding the person and eventually give up attempting to help them because their efforts are always overtly or subtly rejected.

*Manipulative* behaviour is:

- cunning
- indirectly aggressive
- controlling of others in an insidious way, ie by sarcasm or sulking
- two-faced – pleasant to people to their faces but poisonous behind their backs
- devious.

People working with anyone behaving manipulatively feel:

- confused
- angry
- guilty
- frustrated.

Colleagues feel they never know where they stand with a manipulative person, and are annoyed at having to try constantly to work out what is going on.

*Assertive* behaviour is:

- achieving goals without damaging others
- protective of own rights and respectful of others' rights
- feeling good about oneself, having an appropriate level of confidence
- being socially and emotionally expressive
- making one's own choices and taking responsibility for them
- asking directly for needs to be met, while accepting the risk of rejection.

If the people around an assertive person feel confident in themselves they will enjoy these qualities in someone else and feel trust, respect, confidence and pleasure in relating to the person. If they are feeling low in confidence they may feel weak, envious and threatened.

Generally, the colleagues of an assertive person know that they can take her at her word, that she is acting and speaking sincerely and in good faith, that she can cope with justified criticism, accept compliments, and will essentially look after herself.

# Recognising assertive, non-assertive and aggressive behaviour

## Exercise 5

Working either alone or in a group look at the example situations below and see how you would identify the behaviour.

| Situation | Response | Your Answer |
|---|---|---|
| A colleague interrupts you when you are making a call to a customer, you say: | I'd like to finish this phone call, then I'll be with you. | |
| A colleague in another department has volunteered your services without consulting you. You say: | What a nerve! Why didn't you ask me first? There's no way I can help out. I'm up to my eyes as it is. You'll have to manage on your own. | |
| Your boss has sent a memo saying that no more business visits are to be made without her prior agreement. You are unhappy with this and say: | Jane, I'm unhappy with the new arrangement. The way I see it, it takes away my professional judgement. I'd like to discuss it with you. | |

| | |
|---|---|
| A colleague agreed to come to a special meeting but then failed to turn up. You ring him and say: | Well, I suppose it didn't matter that you weren't there. We managed alright without you in the end. |
| A salesperson has been pushing hard for you to buy a pice of equipment. You are not too sure; besides, you had thought of looking at several makes before making a decision. You say: | Well, I guess it's more or less what I'm looking for. I was going to look at other makes but perhaps this will be OK. |
| Your boss is about to leave the office for an important meeting. You need to ask him if you may work at home tomorrow. You say: | I know you're in a rush, John, but I'd like to make a quick request of you. |
| Your secretary is arranging your diary for the day. She asks you what time you will be back in the office. You say: | When you see me walk through that door. |
| You have just written a difficult letter and would like some feedback from a colleague. You say: | I'd like to hear your views on this letter I've written. |

| | |
|---|---|
| One of your colleagues (you don't know which one) forgot to pass on an important message to you. You take this up with your boss. You say: | This department is completely hopeless. They can't even write down a simple message. What are you going to do about it? |

| | |
|---|---|
| The date is being set for the next team meeting. You are keen to attend but the proposed date clashes with another appointment. You say: | Well, all right, it seems to be convenient for everyone else. |

It is important to bear in mind the difference between recognising that someone is behaving in a certain way, and blaming her for it. You can probably visualise yourself as well as your colleagues behaving in many of the less ideal ways described above. Recognising what is going on in the present is the first step towards making the changes we want in the future.

# Section Four

# The Method

## Finding a core phrase

### Exercise 6

Make a list of three or four situations where you would like or would have liked to have been more assertive. Choose any instances when you thought, 'I *wish* I had handled that differently'. For each of these situations, work out a core phrase. Your core phrase expresses exactly what you want to say, without any unnecessary 'padding'.

If you are working in a group, briefly describe the background to your situation. If you are working alone write a paragraph describing the situation.

## Eliminating padding

When you try to express something delicate, difficult or tense, you may find yourself padding it out:

*'I'm really sorry to bother you about this, I know you're terribly busy today ...'*

*'You'll probably think I'm over-reacting, but I just want to say ...'*

*'I'm hopeless with machinery, could you show me ...'*

*'I know you'll be awfully disappointed, but I'm afraid I can't ...'*

This padding takes a lot of the power and impact away from the core phrase by distracting attention from it.

A core phrase without padding would be something like:

*'I'm worried about our lack of progress on this case. Can we arrange a meeting this week to discuss it?'*

*'I haven't come across this type of photocopier before. Could you show me how to operate it?'*

*'Because of the new schedules I don't have time to organise the Christmas party this year. I'd like somebody else to take over that rôle.'*

*'I feel you're not even listening to my views because I'm black and because I'm young.'*

*'I find these posters offensive and I want you to take them down.'*

# Avoiding hooks

### Exercise 7

This exercise is about not getting 'hooked' – that is, not getting pulled into an irrelevant or unproductive argument while you are making your point. You can be effective by:

- showing you hear and understand what the other person is saying
- repeating your core phrase
- working out your fall-back position.

*"Not getting 'hooked'."*

Your fall-back position defines how far you are prepared to compromise towards a workable solution. This helps you to avoid being pushed further than you want to be in your negotiation.

### Showing you hear what the other person is saying:

*'I see you have a hectic week, but I am worried about this case and feel we should discuss it.'*

*'I'm glad you think I organise the Christmas parties beautifully, but I'd like someone else to take on that rôle this year!'*

*'I realise you think I make a fuss about sexism in the office, but I find those posters offensive, and I want them taken down.'*

*'I'm sure I'm not imagining this, and I'm sure my suggestions*

*aren't stupid. I feel you aren't listening to me properly because I'm black and young.'*

# Maintaining your fall-back position

*'I would be prepared to talk about it first thing next Monday.'*
*'I'm certainly happy to pass on all the contacts and phone numbers for caterers.'*

# Taking things further

In some cases, for example in instances of sexist or racist harrassment, no fall-back position is possible because there is little or no room to compromise. It will probably feel appropriate to stand your ground and keep repeating the core phrase. If necessary, be prepared to raise the matter with the appropriate authority, which might be your boss, your union, the Equal Opportunities Commission, or any other group.

Either thinking it through on your own, or in a group getting other people to supply the hook lines, practise fielding these arguments, repeating them to show you have heard and understood and repeating your core phrase.

Common hooks are:

*Argumentative* which might make you lose your temper, eg 'what's happened to your sense of humour?' or 'I should have known better than to leave this to you'.

*Manipulative* which might make you feel guilty, eg 'but we've been looking forward to it so much' or 'well, if you don't do it I really don't know who will, and of course it decreases the junior staff's training opportunities'.

*Apparent 'logic'* which might make you feel confused, eg 'nobody else has ever asked us to arrange it like this', or 'it's a man's world in this profession, my dear, and you must accept its values. If you don't like it you can always leave'.

Notice how you can steady the discussion and continue to make your point clearly by using the technique you have learnt. With practice it ceases to feel rigid, and feels fluid and natural.

### Exercise 8

With the help of partners or a group, or working through in your own mind, try out these rôle-plays, first formulating your core phrase and then practising handling negative hooks assertively. Do not worry about your lack of acting ability! These rôles will come easily; they are close to or parallel with many everyday experiences. Afterwards, share how it feels to use this basic technique.

# Rôle-plays

1   Your colleague, whom you like, is a very able worker, but has a habit of coming into your office and talking to you about gardening. While you are interested in the subject, you are more interested in getting on with your work. Your colleague comes in on a Friday when you are busy.

    Respond assertively.

2   A colleague with whom you work closely has been arriving back very late from lunch for the past few days. This means you cannot get on with the project you are both working on.

    Discuss the situation assertively.

3   You are called to see your senior manager. She tells you that they have reviewed your career and they feel that, in your best interests, you are being appointed to another job

at a more senior level. You do not want this job for several reasons. You do not like the person you will have to work for, the job is very narrow and specialised and does not interest you, etc.

Explain this to the senior manager.

4 You are engaged in a complex exercise with a deadline. Your boss keeps asking you to take care of 'emergencies'. One day, when you are especially busy, your boss enters your office and says to you, 'I know you are busy, but could you see your way to checking this report for me? I have to give it to the editor by mid-day'.

Tell your boss how you feel.

# Finding a 'speaking partner'

You will notice that responding assertively involves keeping steady and level-headed. Choosing to be assertive may involve choosing not to lose your temper, choosing not to become upset, or choosing to contain your feelings in other ways. It is important to make space in another part of your life to let these feelings out! A 'speaking partner' is a good person to share your feelings with – ideally he/she is someone who understands your area of work but does not work in your field, and who does not work in the same organisation as you do. You can make an informal arrangement to meet or talk regularly to give each other support and get rid of any pent-up feelings.

Using assertiveness gives you, in the long run, much *more* opportunity to express and be yourself, and to be powerful and effective. However, there may be incidents in the short-term where you feel your self-expression has been inhibited. This is when your speaking partner is useful. It is also good to have someone with whom you can share your assertiveness successes!

*Section Five*

# The Body and the Voice

The effectiveness of *what* we say is strongly influenced by *how* we say it. Both the quality – speed, pitch and timbre – of our voice, and our posture and body-language either re-inforces or undermines our words.

When they are feeling pressurised or making a controversial point, some people hear their voice go higher, or develop an anxious edge, or drop to a hesitant murmur. Sometimes they speed up as if to get the difficult sentence out as fast as possible, making it difficult for the other person to take in their important point.

Obviously you don't want to start talking in an artificial voice. However, the most effective *kind* of voice to be assertive in is a slowish, lowish delivery, except when you want to be assertively angry, where you might want to get a bit louder. Try out the range and extent of your voice with the following exercise: as with the earlier rôle-plays, do not worry about your acting ability, you will find you can do this easily!

## Exercise 9

### Voices

Say the following sentences out loud in these different ways:

- aggressively
- passively or non-assertively (ie sounding like a martyr or a victim)
- indirectly (sarcastically or sulkily)
- assertively.

Ham it up a bit! Notice the nuances and edges that come into your voice. Do not tell your group which mode you are in; see if they can recognise them.
The sentences are:

1 I'm not happy with this piece of work, and I want it done again.
2 I've got a lot of work to get through and don't want to chat now.
3 I want very much to attend this course, it's most important both for my benefit and the firm's.

Say one more sentence in all four modes, trying when you say it assertively to say it as equal-to-equal, and without sounding patronising or envious.

4 Well done. You managed that extremely well.

If you are in a group share feedback with them on how it felt to speak in the different modes, and how you found your assertive 'voice'. If you are trying these out on your own, reflect on the quality you found in your voice in its assertive mode.

### Body language

Practise becoming aware of the following:

- where you are in relation to the person with whom you are speaking
- what your posture is like
- what your use of gesture is like
- what your facial expression is doing.

*"... where you are in relation to the person with whom you're speaking."*

First, think about your position in the space you are both in: practise taking a couple of seconds when you enter a room to assess this.

Generally speaking, sitting at a much lower level than the other person, or sitting when they are standing, removes some of your power, as does standing talking with someone who is much taller than you. If you are at a much lower level either invite them to sit down too, or make an opportunity to stand up as well and find a comfortable standing position.

If the chair for you to sit in is arranged at an angle that you find awkward, move it so you are sitting at a good workable angle.

How close or how far away is the person to whom you are talking? Do they seem miles away? If so, move a bit closer – you can say, 'I'm just going to move this chair over a bit – you seem a long way away over there'. Alternatively, are they invading your 'personal space', for instance leaning their hand on the back of your chair and breathing down your neck? You do not have to let your space be invaded if you do not wish it to be. Stand up and move away, stand in a different position in relation to the other person where you feel more in control.

Second, consider your posture. In general, the more we can lift the spine and lengthen the back of the neck, release the shoulders and relax the limbs, the more we come across as relaxed and in control. Imagine you are very tired and depressed, and allow your body to collapse as it would in that situation. Notice how you slump and crumple up the front of your body, then jut your chin out and contract your neck. Now, exhale and sit up tall, releasing your shoulders. Notice how much more comfortable your abdomen is because it is not squashed. Notice how your neck and face are more poised. Think of having plenty of room between your ears and your shoulders. The more we twine and plait our limbs the more tense and insecure we appear.

Concentrate on balancing your body *symmetrically,* equal weight in each foot if you are standing, equal weight in each hip if you are sitting, with your head upright and not tilted to one side. Balancing like this will make your body more inclined to arrange itself in a loose and relaxed way, rather than a tight and knotted one. Your words will carry more weight when you have arrived at these habits of relaxed posture.

Such body awareness cannot be learned all at once, so do

not despair if several times a day you notice you are clenching your fists, wringing your hands, or crossing and re-crossing your legs at knees and ankles. Simply relaxing, and sitting or standing balanced and upright whenever it crosses your mind to do so, will gradually make you inhabit your body in a different way.

The third point in our body-language list is gesture. Hand and arm gestures can enhance what we say, but they can also be annoying and distracting. Take time to become aware of what your hands and arms are doing.

Try to keep your hands away from your face. When we are anxious about what we are saying we tend to move our hands up towards the face, sometimes even covering the mouth as though to hold the words in. Slow and expansive hand gestures may be useful, but any sort of fiddling or fidgeting is usually irritating and distracting to the person with whom you are dealing. Continually running your hands through your hair, twisting curls round your fingers, unbending paper clips and so on, does not help you come across as confident and assertive. Added embarrassment arises when the pencil you are fiddling with finally snaps, or the necklace you have been twisting around your fingers breaks, cascading beads across the desk! If you notice a desire to fidget or twitch, exhale deeply and consciously relax your arms and fingers. If you feel really restless and tense, it is probably better to say so, and stand up and pace round the room for a while to use up some of your nervous energy. Awareness and change can not come instantly, so do not despair, but begin to observe yourself and make changes as and when you feel able to do so.

Lastly, facial expression is crucial to communication. It is no good saying something deeply meant and sincere while addressing thin air behind the other person's left shoulder. It is no good expressing anger with an anxious, placatory smile on your face, or trying to make a conciliatory statement wearing a scowl.

Eye contact should be clear but intermittent. An unwavering glare is intimidating, but avoiding the other person's eye completely looks weak. Be careful *not* to avoid the other person's eye when you use any key words or phrases.

When you are being assertive remember to be aware of what your face is doing, and try to make it re-inforce your words and not undermine them.

### Exercise 10

### Personal style

The way we dress and present ourselves says a great deal about our self-esteem and how we see ourselves in an organisation. This may be far more overt in women than in men, but smaller signals and choices mark how men feel about themselves and their prospects as clearly as do more extensive signals in women's style and dress.

*"The way we dress says a great deal about our self esteem ..."*

The purpose of this exercise is to make you more aware of how you present yourself, the signals which your way of presenting yourself sends out about you, and any changes and adjustments you would like to make in this area. Either use the guidelines for a discussion with a partner or a group, or make notes on the points and evolve your own thoughts about the way you choose to look.

1   Describe your favourite item of clothing. It may be something old and comfortable that you have had for ages, or something new, or something which relates to an interest or enthusiasm. Say what you like about it, and what it says about you. If you do not have anything you like, reflect on why this is. If there is something you would like but have not got, describe it, and why you have not got it.

2   Describe how you normally dress at work. What do you like and dislike about it? In what ways is it similar to and in what ways different from your 'favourite' piece of clothing? What do your work clothes and presentation say about you and your skills?

3   Considering the material you have come up with in **1** and **2,** are there any adjustments you would like to make to the signals your personal presentation gives at work? How could you adjust your appearance to help you to be more assertive?

If there are changes you would like to make, consider how and when to put them into practice.

# Section Six

# Criticism and Compliments

## Giving critical feedback in an assertive manner

When it is necessary to give criticism remember this important point: criticise the *behaviour* and *not* the *person*. Say 'that was a daft thing to do' rather than 'you are daft', or 'I'm unhappy with the way you dealt with that' rather than 'you dealt with that badly'.

When we were children, the powerful adults in our lives (parents, teachers, etc) may often have said to us things like 'you are messy', 'you are lazy', 'you are unkind', rather than, 'your room is in a mess and I want you to do something about it', or 'it is time you did some jobs in the house to contribute to the family', or 'that was an unkind thing to do to your sister'. For a child it is hard to make the distinction between particular acts and one's entire self. If an adult tells you 'you are lazy' it is easy to at least partly believe it as a criticism of your entire self.

This of course makes you feel emotional and desperate. You want to argue and resist. The memories of this childhood desperation arise again when you are criticised as an adult if the criticism is of you as a person and not of actions in particular.

If you want to make criticisms which do not make the person feel that sense of desperation, remember this basic point.

With that in mind, think of the criticism you want to make: develop a core phrase and be prepared to repeat it if necessary without getting hooked into a destructive argument, as described in *Section Four*.

Once the criticism has been clearly understood by the other person be ready to initiate a discussion on how to improve things, including setting specific goals for the person being criticised. This way, you leave the session with a clear perception of what your criticism is, and they leave with a clear aim in mind. They can then use the adrenalin the discussion will have generated for something immediate and constructive.

Be careful (see *Section Five* on facial expression) not to confuse your message with a placatory smile or a sneer.


# Dealing with criticism assertively

If you feel panic when you are criticised, remember this probably arises because of blanket criticism of you as a child – ie 'you are clumsy', rather than 'that was a clumsy thing to do'. Try to remind yourself that making one or even a series of mistakes does not mean you are a bad person; it means you made one or a number of mistakes.

If a person makes a blanket criticism about you now, ('I don't like your attitude'; 'You're always difficult about this kind of thing'), use the 'fogging' technique to find out more specifically what she or he really wants to say to you.

## Fogging

Build up a 'fog bank' to defuse the situation by these means:

- do not argue with the criticism, as this would heat things up: say 'maybe I am', or 'perhaps it is'
- prompt more specific material with 'can you say more about what bothers you about this?', 'can you tell me more about what you feel has gone wrong?'.

*"Build up a 'fog bank'."*

Continue fogging until you hear a specific criticism with which you can begin to deal. Here is an example:

*'I don't like your attitude when you're dealing with clients.'*

*'Perhaps my attitude to clients does need looking at. Can you tell me a bit more about what bothers you?'*
*'It's just you, your attitude.'*
*'Can you tell me what it is about my attitude that bothers you?'*
*'It's the way you dress.'*
*'Maybe there is a problem about the way I dress. Can you say what it is about the way I dress that you're concerned about?'*
*'It's too casual.'*
*'Perhaps it is too casual. Could you say what it is that strikes you as too casual?'*
*'I just don't think it's appropriate for women professionals to wear trousers when they're interviewing clients.'*

By going through the fogging process the specific point at issue becomes clear.

# Dealing with valid and invalid criticism

When we hear a valid criticism we must temper the initial sinking of the heart by reminding ourselves that specific mistakes or stupidities do not make us an out-and-out useless person.

Accepting valid criticism assertively involves saying the criticism back to the critic to show that you have heard it clearly and accept it:

*'I agree. I have made a mess of this project.'*
*'You're right. I should not have lost my temper with that client.'*
*'Yes, I did rush through the points too fast at the meeting.'*

If you *want* to apologise, do so, but do not go on and on and pad it out.

*'I'm so sorry that I was rude. I was under a lot of pressure that day but I realise that's no excuse.'*

When you have clearly accepted and 'owned' the criticism, you might want to add a positive sentence looking at how things can be improved.

*'I agree. I have made a mess of this project. Can you suggest what we can do to start recovering the situation?'*
*'You're right. I should not have lost my temper with that client. What do you think is the most effective way of apologising and regaining his trust?'*
*'Yes, I did rush through the points too fast at the meeting. I'm working on my tendency to panic and rush in meetings, and I think I am slowly beginning to improve.'*

Accepting a valid criticism calmly, and looking straightaway for opportunities for constructive action, will usually keep the whole situation calm and positive, rather than it being a source of conflict and distress. It also, paradoxical though it may seem at first, maintains your personal dignity and power far more effectively than resisting a criticism which you know in your heart is true, simply because you fear giving any ground.

### Exercise 11

You may find yourself in situations where the atmosphere is uncomfortable and you do not understand why: perhaps a colleague is being less forthcoming than usual, or you sense a general disapproval in the air. If you can prompt valid criticisms from the people concerned, you may be able to find out what is wrong.

# Prompting valid criticism – rôle-plays

1   You were not given a salary increase while others on your level were. You want to ask your boss the reason why.

2  During your performance appraisal, the person inter-viewing you makes comments such as: your staff's morale is low; you are poorly organised; and your communications are bad. You know these aren't the real problems. Find out what the issues actually are.

3  One of your colleagues seems reluctant to discuss a particular issue or problem; he used to be quite happy to discuss things, but he seems to have changed. You don't understand why.

If the criticism you are hearing is invalid, you do not have to agree with it. To disagree assertively with an invalid criticism it is important to repeat the criticism back to the critic, to make sure they know you heard and understood it clearly. Keep your voice level and steady and make sure your body language and your expression re-inforce what you are saying:

*'No, I don't agree with that. I have not been an unreliable co-worker.'*

*'No, that isn't correct. I did check all the details before the letters went out.'*

*'No, I really don't feel I am unapproachable with my staff. I don't think that's the case.'*

If the invalid criticism makes you angry or upset, you may want to report the feeling, making an 'I' statement ('I feel upset about that') not a 'you' statement ('you've upset me now').

*'I'm angry at the implications of what you're saying. I don't accept at all that I don't have the staff's best interests at heart.'*

*'I'm amazed that you feel I'm not pulling my weight; you know I have worked many extra hours on this case, and I feel quite clear that I have put my best efforts into it.'*

*'I feel upset about what you're saying. I do not accept that I am a troublemaker.'*

Assertively countering a criticism which you consider to be

invalid makes a clear point without generating extra tension. It feels far more powerful than yelling back aggressively, or collapsing into the martyred victim pose.

Sometimes we do not know whether a criticism is valid or not. If we try to check it against our own perceptions we can often feel confused and really do not know whether it is true or not. If it is possible in the circumstances, report this and ask for time to consider:

*'Well, I'm surprised to hear your opinion, and I'm really not sure what I feel about it myself. Can I come back to you when I've thought it over?'*

Look back to Exercise 3 in Section Two.

Some criticisms (valid or invalid) may particularly upset you because they contain material which is very sensitive for you. It is useful to identify any areas of criticism which are particularly upsetting to you, and to be careful to respond clearly using your assertive skills. (Bear in mind that you can discharge your emotions to your speaking partner later.)

If a particularly unsettling piece of criticism comes your way it is useful to remind yourself of your strengths before moving on to making your assertive response. This will help you to keep your equilibrium.

# Positive feedback

To give positive feedback in an assertive manner, think of being clear and specific, and of leaving out any anxious padding such as 'I hope you don't mind me saying this ...' and 'if I may I'd just like to say ...':

*'I've been most impressed with your work this week.'*
*'That was a tricky interview. I thought you were very sensitive.'*
*'It can't have been easy to complete that case in those conditions. Well done.'*

In a highly competitive world it can feel risky to give someone a compliment, as though re-inforcing them might take away from yourself. It is useful to develop an attitude which enables you to feel that it is safe to acknowledge and enjoy other people's strengths as well as your own.

If you want to give someone a compliment be aware of your voice: watch out for a patronising ring or an envious edge (sometimes if you hear that edge creeping in you can defuse it by mentioning it, 'I actually feel quite envious of the way you managed that').

Perhaps you are feeling so aware of the nasty internal politics of the organisation in which you work that the thought of being open and honest seems like a bad joke. While of course you may need to be careful how and where you are open and therefore vulnerable, bear in mind that especially when you are leading or supervising a team, positive feedback is crucial. A reflex and habitual 'good, well done', is soon disregarded, but being specific about what you are praising or complimenting makes it a powerful force in motivating staff.

Receiving compliments so that they are a genuine positive help to you may need some thought and practice. Points to remember are:

- accept the praise, don't deny it
- don't divert the credit or deny your own rôle
- don't rush your acceptance of the positive feedback
- enjoy the affirmation without feeling guilty.

It is very easy to deny the praise completely ('Oh, it was nothing', or 'Oh, I find that kind of thing easy, it's no problem'), or to divert the credit ('Oh, it was the team actually, not me'). While it is important to give credit where it is deserved – and nothing infuriates and demoralises a workforce more thoroughly than seeing a senior member of the hierarchy take the credit for work which they actually did themselves – it is possible to say 'thank you, I'm glad you feel it went well. The team supported me excellently, too'.

If you feel embarrassed and reserved about taking in positive feedback properly, you will be inclined to rush over the praise: 'Yes, well, good. Now, the next important point we have to deal with is ...' If someone pays you a compliment or gives you some positive feedback, consciously miss a beat before you answer. Let the words hang in the air for a moment!: '(pause) ... thank you. I thought it went well, and I'm pleased that you did too.' Remember that there is nothing bigheaded about enjoying praise – so do not feel guilty about it!

With our growing awareness of sexism in the workplace compliments on appearance pose a particular problem. If you are a man complimenting a woman on her appearance you need to think through what other signals you are giving with

*"Accept the praise, don't deny it."*

the compliment. Is it really a spontaneous and friendly comment or does it contain elements which are patronising, sexist, and (unwelcomely) flirtatious? Would you say the same kind of thing to a male colleague who came in in a new suit or haircut? If not, maybe you should think about either being more responsive to the appearance of male colleagues, and/or being careful to be aware what the subtexts are with women colleagues. Men often say things like, *'I'm not sure if I'm allowed to say to you that you look nice'*, but it is their responsibility to sort out whether they want to say something or not, and not the woman's responsibility to make them feel all right about it.

For the moment anyway, comments that might have been thought of as habitual courtesy or harmless gallantry should be thought through in terms of what they mean about power in the workplace.

# Section Eight

# Stress Management in High Tension Situations

There are times when we all feel our adrenalin rise like mercury climbing the column of a thermometer: for example, during a negotiation where the outcome is of extreme importance to us; being dismissed or dismissing someone else; confronting sexism or racism; or dealing with severe critical feedback. Even reading the list may have slightly increased your pulse rate! When tension is high there are various aspects of assertiveness which can be useful.

First, be aware of your physiology. Episodes of acute tension produce an increased pulse rate, increased volume of breathing, increased perspiration, increased activity in the gut, and sometimes shaking. These are all your animal 'fight or flight' mechanisms, making you ready to be more effective in physical combat, and are nothing to be embarrassed about or ashamed of.

Because most conflicts in the workplace are not resolved by physical combat, you have to use the resources your body puts at your disposal in a different way – but they are resources nonetheless. The increase in circulation of oxygenated blood makes you more alert and more able to think clearly and quickly. Because you do not need the increased muscular strength generated by clenching or shaking, you may wish consciously to lengthen and relax your muscles. If your hands are shaking you could acknowledge it – 'I'm so tense I've started to shake' – or if you do not want it to show rest your hands in your lap and breathe deeply, imagining you are exhaling through your fingertips. This usually helps.

Abdominal discomfort reflects our animal self getting ready to make itself as light as possible by getting rid of all its waste products. It helps to know that everyone finds acute tension highly laxative! You will be more comfortable if you can go to the toilet before a high-tension interview, but if you can not or if it arises unexpectedly simply be aware why you feel the way you do, and relax your abdominal muscles, breathing deeply and steadily.

*"... everyone finds acute tension highly laxative!"*

Women *and* men may dread the onset of weeping as a sign of weakness, although it is a natural enough physiological reaction to shock and distress. If your throat is closing up and tears seem inevitable, it is sometimes useful to say so: *'I can feel that I'm going to cry in a minute or two'*; or to go out of the room and try to steady yourself; *'Excuse me for a few moments. I am going outside to calm down'*.

When you get out of the room consciously relax your shoulders and breathe deeply, being particularly aware of the breath *out*. Remind yourself of your strengths (see page 7). Remind yourself that you *will* get through the situation, just as you have survived all sorts of other things in the past.

If you are dealing with someone who is crying, see if you can acknowledge their tears without feeling coerced by them:

*'I can see this is distressing you, and it's a very unpleasant and difficult situation for us both. Would you like a few moments to take a few deep breaths and calm down?'*

You might want openly to declare the high tension in the situation by saying something like:

- this is difficult for both of us
- this is very important to both of us
- I am extremely angry
- this is a shocking situation
- this is distressing for both of us
- I've got a serious complaint to make.

It might be strategically necessary to be less open, however, and to work on maintaining your own strength and equilibrium.

# Disarming anger

If you want to decrease the electrical charge in an encounter a number of points may be useful:

- a change of venue
- active listening and empathy
- showing you want a win–win solution.

### A change of venue

Simply walking along a corridor and moving into a different room may 'unstick' the tension between two people. Someone who is very angry quickly feels suffocated in one place. If you are dealing with someone who is very angry whom you want to calm down, go outside and walk with them while you talk, if you work near anywhere suitable. A lot of tension can be discharged this way.

### Active listening

If you want to calm down a very angry person, say 'tell me *exactly* what is wrong', and listen actively, with plenty of eye contact, nods, and 'yesses', but do not interrupt or argue at all until you feel their angry energy starting to ease up. Make plenty of space for their anger and be an empathetic listener, but keep your own breathing steady and do not allow yourself to be 'invaded' by the anger.

### Showing you want a win–win situation

Once the pace of the angry energy has slowed, show that you want to arrive at a solution which will be workable for both of you: *'Let's look at this together, a point at a time'*.

# Standing your ground

You may be the person who is angry and feel a need to express that anger fully and to stand your ground. Stay in touch with your anger and your right to be angry. Shout or cry if you want to, but be aware that in that case you are making a choice to behave in a way that may be labelled 'unreasonable' or 'hysterical' later on.

Stick to your core phrase. You can still be quite fierce without spilling over into the undesirable aggressive mode:

*'This is a serious complaint that I am making. I insist that we take it further.'*

*'I am very angry about this decision being made behind my back. I want to know exactly why it happened.'*

*'This is the third time you have turned in a very bad piece of work. I want to know what your reasons are for what appears to be a complete lack of effort.'*

# The aftermath

After a particularly nasty scene, remember the importance of self-affirmation (Exercises 1 and 2) and use the support of your speaking partner (see Section Four) to get yourself back into a steady frame of mind. If you work in a job where there are constant traumatic interviews (for instance, Housing Benefit Offices), consider setting up a procedure to give each other emergency support whenever needed.

# Section Nine

# Saying 'No'

When you say 'no' you are refusing the request, not rejecting the person. If you can keep that clear in your mind, you will find saying no much easier to do.

In making an assertive refusal, the key is in the core phrase without padding. Think how often it is possible to get into a tangle over things like:

*'I would love to of course but unfortunately it's impossible ...'*
*'I'm really sorry to let you down, I know you've been counting on me, but I just can't help ...'*

When you say 'no':

- you need not apologise unless you want to apologise; and
- you need not explain why your answer is 'no' unless it is professionally necessary to explain or unless you want to explain.

For example, it is all right to say:

*'No, I won't take on that project.'*

If you want to express regret, do so:

*'No, I won't take on that project, although I'm sorry to miss the opportunity.'*

If you want to explain your reasons, or you feel you are obliged to explain for professional reasons, add:

*'No, I won't take on that project, although I'm sorry to miss the opportunity. It's not in my main field and it would be unrealistic to think I would get through the background reading this year.'*

Think how much clearer this is to say and to hear than:

*'Oh, I'm sorry, I'm hopeless in that area, I'd never manage it, and I'm so pushed for time. I'm really sorry – however are you going to manage if I don't?'*

In the first example you have stated your position clearly and positively and with self-respect. In the second you are running yourself down needlessly and also being ambiguous and leaving the door open – you might still be persuaded because you are clearly feeling guilty.

Say your core phrase calmly and clearly, and have your fall-back position clearly in mind if you are prepared to negotiate to some extent. Be ready to repeat the core phrase if necessary and look out for the same sort of hooks (manipulative, argumentative, irrelevant logic) as described in *Section Four*. Be aware of what your face and body language are doing. Try not to squirm, or to smile anxiously.

When you have said 'no' clearly and it has been heard and accepted, do not hang around. Physically go away or change the subject completely. Do not hover, saying things like, 'is that all right?', 'are you sure you can manage now?', 'I'm sorry, it's just one of those things', or 'I hope you won't think badly of me because of this'. This will completely undermine your refusal. Make a clean start on a new subject or get right away.

People worry that saying no clearly will offend colleagues and friends, but this is rarely the case. It is much easier to know where you stand if someone says a clear 'no' to you. If they say a messy 'fudged' no, on reflection you are not too sure whether they meant it, and you certainly are not sure what their reasons or feelings about it are. Try this out in the following exercise.

## Exercise 12

Discuss with a partner or a group, or make notes on the following:

- An occasion recently where you received a clear 'no'. What were the circumstances? How did you feel about the refusal, and the person who made the refusal? How did you react, and how did you continue in that situation?
- An occasion recently where you received a messy, unclear or fudged 'no'. What were the circumstances? How did you feel about the unclear refusal and the person who made it? How did you react and how did you continue in that situation?
- An occasion recently where you said a clear 'no'. What were the circumstances? How did it feel to you to say 'no' clearly? How did the other person react? What happened next?
- An occasion recently where you said a messy or fudged 'no'. What were the circumstances? How did you feel saying an unclear 'no'? How did the other person react? What happened next?

Share any information and insights you get from these reflections on the differences between a clear 'no' and an equivocal 'no'.

## Exercise 13

### Rôle-play

With a partner or a group, or making notes and working on your own, try saying 'no' in these rôle-plays. If you have a partner or group for support, get them to act out hooking you.

1  You are asked to visit a client to brief them on a forthcoming project. Although you are pleased to be asked, you do not feel you know enough about this project and do not want to make the visit alone.

2  Some work should have been sent out to a client. You know it is still unfinished in the office. Your boss has asked you to ring the client to tell him it is in the post. You do not want to be asked to lie on someone else's behalf.

3  You have a desk by a pleasant window in the office. A colleague says he is having problems with headaches and eyestrain and needs to be closer to a natural source of light. He asks if you will swap desks with him. You do not want to.

# Section Ten

# Range and Limitations

After working through the exercises in this book you will have a sense of the scope of assertiveness. If you have tried out or thought through the rôle-plays you will have seen their applications in dealing with conflict with colleagues; confronting racism and sexism; negotiation; being heard in meetings; and dealing with personnel issues. It will have become clear to you that assertiveness is a vital resource for helping you to work on good time-planning or good stress management.

There are, of course, limitations. One is not always quick enough to evolve a core phrase, or aware enough of how another person's personality is hooking into old negative patterns of ones own. Self-esteem has its off-days and some situations are just too complex to understand except in retrospect. Even so, the habits of mind, the growth in positive attitude, the clear speaking, and self-respect which using assertiveness promotes can be a very positive influence in our working lives.

Assertiveness is not an obligation: you do not have to use it day in, day out, or feel loyalty towards it as a philosophy, or feel guilty if you choose not to be assertive. Neither is it a panacea: situations may exist where it will not 'work' or 'win' but there will be few situations where it does not help. Assertiveness is an excellent addition to your repertoire of working skills, and it will enhance your performance and your effectiveness at work.

# Bibliography

## Assertiveness
*Self Assertion for Women:* Pamela Butler, Harper and Rowe, 1981
*A Woman in Your Own Right:* Anne Dickson, Quartet, 1982

## Harrassment and Assault
*Women and Harrassment at Work:* Nathalie Hadjifotiou, Pluto Press, 1983
*Against Our Will:* Susan Brownmiller, Penguin, 1977

## Coping with Aggression and Violence
*Beating Aggression:* Diana Lamplugh, Weidenfeld Paperback, 1988
*Stand Your Ground:* Kaleghl Quinn, Optima, 1983
*Her Wits About Her:* Denise Caignon and Gail Groves, The Women's Press, 1987

## Multiple Commitments
*Managing Two Careers:* Paddy O'Brien, Sheldon, 1989

## Personal Growth
*In Our Own Hands:* Ernst and Goddison, The Women's Press, 1981
*Living with the Sphinx:* Ernst and Maguire, The Women's Press, 1987
*Towards a New Psychology of Women:* Jean Baker Miller, Penguin, 1976

## Health
*Our Bodies Ourselves:* Boston Women's Health Collective, Penguin, 1978, 2nd ed. 1990

# Relaxation

*Stretch and Relax:* Maxine Tobias and Mary Stewart, Dorling Kindersley, 1985
*The Sensual Body:* Lucy Liddell, Unwin Hyman, 1987
*Stress Management:* Charlesworth and Nathan, Corgi, 1986

# Equal Opportunities: the work of the Pepperell Department

The Pepperell Department helps develop individual potential and organisational effectiveness through the practice of equal opportunities and the management of change. It works in all areas of race, gender, and disability and believes that helping people be more effective makes good business sense. Their equal opportunity and career development courses include:

- making equal opportunities happen, putting policy into practice
- fair selection recruitment and development
- equal opportunities officers' forum
- improving personal effectiveness: an assertiveness workshop
- counselling skills for managers
- divided loyalties
- career and management development skills for women
- the Pepperell development course for women
- power and influence in organisations.

# Improving personal effectiveness: an assertiveness workshop

The purpose of this Pepperell Department course is to:

- look at your own behaviour in various situations
- increase your skills or assertiveness when dealing with these situations
- improve your confidence and skill when handling difficult behaviour from others.

It is designed for anyone wanting to improve the way they deal with situations and people at work. The programme covers the following:

- With the help of discussions and small group exercises, course members will develop personal awareness, and practise the skills of behaving assertively.
- Managing relationships: what is assertive behaviour? How it can help with awkward moments.
- Developing the skills of assertion to enable you to control the responses of others.
- Individual goal setting: areas for personal development are identified and the assertive steps you can begin to take are examined.

- Maintaining self-assertion: when dealing with difficult people what are the skills you must develop?
- Putting it into practice: individual action plans to build on your assertive skills and maintain your position of confidence.

Details of this and other Pepperell courses can be obtained from
The Industrial Society
Robert Hyde House
48 Bryanston Square
London
W1H 7LN
Tel: 071-262-2401